First World War
and Army of Occupation
War Diary
France, Belgium and Germany

27 DIVISION
Headquarters, Branches and Services
Royal Army Ordnance Corps
Deputy Assistant Director Ordnance Services
1 June 1915 - 30 November 1915

WO95/2256/4

The Naval & Military Press Ltd
www.nmarchive.com
Published in association with The National Archives

Published by

The Naval & Military Press Ltd

Unit 10 Ridgewood Industrial Park,

Uckfield, East Sussex,

TN22 5QE England

Tel: +44 (0) 1825 749494

www.naval-military-press.com

www.nmarchive.com

This diary has been reprinted in facsimile from the original. Any imperfections are inevitably reproduced and the quality may fall short of modern type and cartographic standards.

© **Crown Copyright**
Images reproduced by permission of The National Archives, London, England, 2015.

Contents

Document type	Place/Title	Date From	Date To
Heading	WO95/2256/4		
Heading	27th Division Divl Toops D.A.D.O.S. Jun-Nov 1915		
Miscellaneous	??		
Heading	War Diary of D.A.D.O.S. 27th Division From 1-30th June 1915 (Volume 1)		
War Diary	Croix Du Bac	01/06/1915	30/06/1915
Heading	27th Division D.A.D.O.S. 27th Division Vol II From 1st To 30th July 1915		
War Diary	Croix Du Bac	01/07/1915	30/07/1915
Heading	War Diary of D.A.D.O.S. 27th Division From 1st August 1915 To 31st August 1915 (Volume III)		
War Diary	Croix Du Bac	01/08/1915	31/08/1915
Heading	War Diary of D.A.D.O.S. 27th Division From 1st September 15 To 30th September 1915 (Volume IV)		
War Diary	Croix Du Bac	01/09/1915	15/09/1915
War Diary	Merris	16/09/1915	18/09/1915
War Diary	Warfusee	19/09/1915	20/09/1915
War Diary	Mericourt	21/09/1915	30/09/1915
Heading	D.A.D.O.S. 27th Div. Oct. 1915 Vol V		
War Diary	Mericourt	01/10/1915	25/10/1915
War Diary	Bovelles	25/10/1915	31/10/1915
Heading	D.A.D.O.S. 27th Div Nov. Vol VI		
Heading	War Diary of D.A.D.O.S. 27th Division From 1st To 30th November 1915 Vol 2		
War Diary	Bovelles	01/11/1915	15/11/1915
War Diary	Marseilles	16/11/1915	30/11/1915

WO 95/2256/4

27TH DIVISION
DIVL TROOPS

D.A.D.O.S.
JUN - NOV 1915

Army Form C. 2118.

WAR DIARY
or
INTELLIGENCE SUMMARY.
(Erase heading not required.)

Hour, Date, Place	Summary of Events and Information	Remarks and references to Appendices
	Confidential. War Diary of D.A.D.O.S. 27th Division from 1 - 30th June 1915 (Volume 1.)	

Instructions regarding War Diaries and Intelligence Summaries are contained in F.S. Regs., Part II. and the Staff Manual respectively. Title pages will be prepared in manuscript.

17 JUL 1915

WAR DIARY or INTELLIGENCE SUMMARY.

(Erase heading not required.)

Army Form C. 2118.

Hour, Date, Place	Summary of Events and Information	Remarks and references to Appendices
CROIX DU BAC. 1-6-15	6.5. Smoke helmets issued to each Battalion. Two telescopic Rifles received from OC 3rd Corps Troops. also 28 Hand bells for use in trenches and Maxim gun shield for trial.	Hand bells issued 7 to each Bde. 1 Tele.scopic rifle to Bde & to 82nd
" 2-6-15	Attended conference of GOCs at A.Q.H.Q. office 3rd Corps. 12 noon. Received 15,000 prs of goggles to be issued by the Corps for use in combating obnoxious gases. also 15,000 No. up bottles, 1,293 lbs R.J.A. A.C. solution and the 100gm R.J. Anti-18 Pr. to Redhead (STEENWERKE) recovered after predawn round YPRES and was supplied every battle having been received from base. A further 65 Smoke helmets issued to each Battalion. Vickers 10n 3rd Corps and average from repair of ordered travelling cookers when they broke.	
" 3-6-15	Ordered transfer of underseat NK.II from 4th R.B. to 7th Battery R.F.A. 4th R.B. having received same to be T lock and received on loan from 10n 5th Corps. 11 trench ordered mortars U cut 8 trans- 8 trench mortars of reserves to be allotted to the 3 Brigades also 10 Rifles with BSA target sights. Despatched Gleadale to Paris w/ 4 Inf.Off. sent from Armentière. Apples for treatment of 100 received to 3rd Corps.	
" 4-6-15	Important to, Rej to Paymaster Paris. Issued 24 Damaged rifles to R.E. for 2 Army Workshops Red S. Gunner rifle 11 Rend'd from 88 & 7 Bde & 1 Rifle Grenade Discharges from 82nd Bde & 630 a.m. Received 7 no Police (1 N.C.O) from 88 3rd Corps. Army shop away to autric in tubes wy to Charles Bn? 1st Inf. Bde moved shop away to autric in tubes wy to Charles Bn? workshop. Report on Strobe cleaning Chambers to 5th Corps; from all reports on by Bde.	

WAR DIARY
or
INTELLIGENCE SUMMARY

(Erase heading not required.)

Army Form C. 2118.

Hour, Date, Place	Summary of Events and Information	Remarks and references to Appendices
CROIX DU BAC. 5-6-15	Informed by Signals that no order could be sent by wire & must be sent by DRLS to B"Army: Note Generally unpunctuated. Priority & they must be accepted. Telescope aft: 4371 returned by 1st Jam & 60's filling out file broken.	
6-6-15	Visited BDes H.Q's. issued Refills also BSA Magnify. sights 2 Brig H.B.De 2 " — 2 C B. — 2 B. — 1000 Rounds Pistol Amo received for 3rd Corps — allotted equally to BDes.	
7-6-15	Received from 3rd Corps HQ 10,000 x P Map for projectors. 300 V gilded Pack wagons — 250 prs of braces for pair of LP goggles 30,000 rds ammo about received for Ammo. 290 articles handed over by 6 Div to 91 NZ Bde return to RETAIL STRAZEELE thro Inspect R. Ruth.	250 rds to 8,00 Corps Troops — throughly inspected 375
8-6-15	Issued 2 Vickers guns to 18th Can. 6.0 Bde By 61: Return of 1 Man Range Finders to 3 Corps in S/c Accessory transport & adjust 1 in use scale 1 per Battery 62 & Bn. Arranged for local repair of Scale Holland uniform 1 set of No 2. application to Corps for whom articles for use in general of Battalion.	
9-6-15	20 Rifles with BSA Magnify. sights read for 3rd Corps allotted 5 each BDe also 1 Rifle Telescopic allotted 19 & 71 BDe Attended conference 7000's at the DG 9th Corps. Issued Panel 11 Gp. defence off army Fld also 1 Bicycle.	

WAR DIARY or INTELLIGENCE SUMMARY

Army Form C. 2118.

Hour, Date, Place	Summary of Events and Information	Remarks and references to Appendices
CROIX DU BAC. 10-6-15	Based on Unserviceable Blankets - all 19th Bde Gps. as issued 178 & to Belgians. Visited 2nd Army Workshops ARMENTIÈRES. Return rendered to 3rd Corps of Trench Howitzers & Py.	to 4 Mk III 2 " III x
" 11-6-15	4 R.BDe reports obtained cycles. (Instead) had been arranged out at well off unit not known but used. 2 German Rifles and 1 Bayonet sent to base. 1450 Smoke Helmets received. 7 Hand bells (trumpets) from 82 "to 80 G.T.BDe	
" 12-6-15	Indented on base for 21,000 Respirators. An 2. 18,700 Helmets to complete reserve. Reqd 30 Rifle Periscopes (Provided locally) from 3rd Corps. Issued 8 G. and BDe except 19 retained ar. Application put forward for 2 more headquarters to Corps HQ. 1st Cambridge Regt reports transfer of 2 transport 9 R. Scots completed. Latter Regt. now in possession of 4 Maxims. Sent out of Bethnal Gun stores to 9 DOS 2nd Army and the Bag on 26th am. 1 wanted also Klaxon.	
" 13-6-15	Put up letter GS Corps re weakness of Travelling Kettle echelon. Reported by wire to all concerned that 12 Howitzer BDe cavalry of H.Q. and 4.3°.87 Batteries fired 6" Gun on 15th and that A Battery 53rd BDe 2 A Battery 65 BDe (Howitzers) each entrained on 1st BDe A.C. had joined Div. Transport convoy of 2 limbered Wagons read from 4 Division for 9 R. Scots for the 2 extra machine guns.	

WAR DIARY or INTELLIGENCE SUMMARY

Army Form C. 2118.

Hour, Date, Place	Summary of Events and Information	Remarks and references to Appendices
CROIX DU BAC. 14-6-15	20.50 Smoke Helmets received from Base. Purchased 127 Sanity Drinkers for 131 Battery. I reply to rpa. from 3rd Corps letter putup recommending cases of 3 Hd Tents to survived Anti Gl. a 3 ple pickup ing game.	
" 15-6-15	11.50 Smoke Helmets received for Base. 2 German Rifles received for R. Irish Fusiliers. Recommended steps wrep to Battery. Hul. 4 Pokey g. 81. + 8 of enamelled shells labels by Battalion makers of presentscale of 12 Pkts of enamelled. Letter put up to 3rd Corps Apph — J for detaps. put tery on quadrants of C.R.A. P (Walls prepared on fub to by and LD 21.g.	
" 16-6-15	Arranged for hire of workshop until Trailer from "A" Battery HAZEBROUCK at ERQUINGHEM by for mean Divisional Armourers shops at 2 places per day. Attended conference of Stoes at 3rd Corps. 5.8 Verlo for concealing from receives o allotted 126 and BDe 210 GRA —	
" 17-6-15	31.50 Helmets received. all arrived to unit. Hot peals reserves of alloted arty. 2 Vickers guns to Garrison allotted to Tr. bridge, 3 complete Lewgun. No. 69.17 Ptl. Cochrane 3' KRR arrived as cool for Detachan all.	
" 18-6-15	3.000 Respirators 0.12.00 Smoke Helmets rec'd. hy Battn call Battaues of R.E entered. completes up to present now 3.1" Trench Battery joined Garrison from Trench Mortar School. BERTEN strength 25. 4 Vickers 40 M.R. Used Mortars.	

Army Form C. 2118.

WAR DIARY
or
INTELLIGENCE SUMMARY.
(Erase heading not required.)

Instructions regarding War Diaries and Intelligence Summaries are contained in F. S. Regs., Part II. and the Staff Manual respectively. Title pages will be prepared in manuscript.

Hour, Date, Place	Summary of Events and Information	Remarks and references to Appendices
CROIX DU BAC 19-6-15.	Patrol billets for use of 6 Sergeants escorts etc employed at Divisional Baths. Indents taken to 2nd & 3rd Divs. re ordering Ammunition & shops. 49 Vela recd from O/C 3rd Corps Patrol allotted 10 to each Div e 7 GHQ. Same as pattern previously used.	(Not approved)
" 20-6-15.	10.30 South Methods Fixed. Patrols applied to 2nd Army to produce past 1000 tyres at 1.30 pm like pt showing one of 2nd Auto Coy. Same arrangements as for ordering lamps previously in use.	
" 21-6-15.	Purchased 127 J. andy Bombs for 67 M. Battery.	Will off Patrol from 2nd Army
" 22-6-15.	Ammunition shop a/c to Test result 5.67 for the Date. Obtained 50 Rifles from No 2 Clearing Station. Indent sent in for hundred. 25 local pattern side letters received from 3rd Corps fitted drives in trenches in varying places. Purchased 210 small Vehicle tool tracks for repair.	
" 23-6-15.	Attended conference of 5000 at 2nd Corps. Re L. of 3/5 of 2nd Army. To effect actions for repair of Vehicles inside. Sent a M. K. III hand Roller 4 R to same lorry to Bklgn Gate Plus with new Davis Mechanic in which has been lost in operations round YPRES. Purchased 45 Bombs 5 m 7 f m 11th Battery.	
" 24-6-15.	Represented 2nd 3rd Corps in status. Re M. Gun. Is was for to take life. Many of a Mill not be carried on in work. Rejects to vehicles on to fit bed also Patrol. Lorry. Column test ask accepted all rifles. Something not venti takes later 50y photo on a sleep carely obtained substitute. Received 3000 small Vehicle template (prossure) of stephene U.	

WAR DIARY
or
INTELLIGENCE SUMMARY.
(Erase heading not required.)

Army Form C. 2118.

Hour, Date, Place	Summary of Events and Information	Remarks and references to Appendices
CROIX DU BAC 25-6-15.	No station Base. Then will necessitate carrying Rabbit hits a double Distribution this evening. Very inconvenient when on Journey of 20 miles. 17th Field Coy R.E. returned Wagon. Pole - Stone broken across my Trip. Only received instrument. Purchased 5 Grindery brushes from 2nd Bridging Team. Reported to 3rd Corps estimate of money taken 34" required for H.Q. Horses viz 130 Brig. Hdts Col. already have these. Sent A.R. on N.C.Os who to be by JR/5 to O/C Base 2nd & 3rd Echelon	
26-6-15.	Despatched 72 Rifles & 16 Bay: to 1st Base with Sworn Statement from Notifying Horses in Supply Col & Note to Division also consignment of blankets clothing and Boots. To P.a.U. who all had been withdrawn from Troops. 6712 Pte Kelly returned in 6 Days leave to Tidworth on 4th July 5-15.	
27-6-15.	Base return Horseshoes on last Week's Return. Went instead of Ammunition Well cancelled upset current work. Steward had three Stewards sons. Wire received from R.T.D. 3rd Corps Railhead stating hail had been the all loaded by Noon daily. This will necessitate Dumping stores from Henry at Detraining Point. It might be needful in winter weather to cover wagon well.	
28-6-15.	Recovery in Carry number of small Rabbits with Butter-hoe Dons for repair. ASP all 697 received from 11th battalion. Arranged for 1 Boy also Trainer Detail also this is necessary to enable lorries to get to Railhead all detail voices being overloaded in one lorry.	

WAR DIARY
or
INTELLIGENCE SUMMARY.
(Erase heading not required.)

Army Form C. 2118.

Hour, Date, Place	Summary of Events and Information	Remarks and references to Appendices
CROIX DU BAC. 29-6-15.	Received 4 Pairs of SHOETACK J.S. Boots to kill also. 1 Sig Wr Pendulum to fury Rifle grenade antiprover pattern J DOS in Army called. Received letter from Bde No MRI Maxim connected Bowels available. Suggested grin shortd be withdrawn from unit crosshead. Received 1000 bags from S.O.S of Helmets	7th R Scots.
30-6-15.	Attended weekly BDO's conference at 3rd Corps. Put out to Culvert bags received to-day to have lips sewn on etc. Produced 8 Cyprus Hay for Cane mines and Sandy Number for 3rd Cy Train. Called for reports from units as number of Gumboots recommended to none for unditrees. Report to 3rd Corps. Re BSA sights Rifle (majority Levis) favorable: appendix. Sent 9.2.25 p.o.j Dougle withdrawn for units envy training Sack Helmets to 3rd Corps Rs. Provisgnts appointment of Pte Tuck to officer Corp withpay from 15-6-15. Corporal Vessel by of Lce Corp Kelly 6712 to Private from 29-4-15 reed army forecasting portion furnished appointment war given.	

Lieut Col
3rd R S
30/6/15
27 Lys

27th Division

121/6443

DADOS. 27th Division

Vol II

From 1st to 30th July 1915

WAR DIARY
INTELLIGENCE SUMMARY
(Erase heading not required.)

Army Form C. 2118.

Hour, Date, Place	Summary of Events and Information	Remarks and references to Appendices
CROIX DU BAC 1-7-15.	Report put up to 3rd Corps re Hauline rifle received for trial favourably reported on by units. Amongst one Brigade preferred the B.S.A. Mark III. Orders received from 3rd Corps to demand 2 Nosebags from Base and transfer 2 Vickers from 1st Cambridge Rt. 12th Division on receipt. 10 Catapults received from Base.	
2-7-15.	1 Catapult issued to 81st and one to 82nd Bde. O.4. to Gd. 1-by-7 pm. was at Bombing School. Our Supply Col. relieved the short Rifle of the 2nd Gunner ptc. Lorry and we issued with long rifles. 4 Rifles short received from Motor Car Drivers of same. Returned to base until telephoned by gd. Col. Letter put up to Corps, asking for regime entry. Mauser converted 7 mm. 1 Kit in possession of 9 th R.S. costs.	
3-7-15.	Reply to 3rd Corps (in reply to enquiry as to number of gun locks, magazines etc in use to Division forwarded) 16.8.00 infantry of 1st 2nd Rd Bde and 2/3 for infantry of R.E. tel received 20-18 pm in which case units would be 25,000 including 1/4 Div Arty. Promotion of Capt 5.5. Dickenson to rank of Lieut notified by 2nd Army, dated 18-5-15. Gazette of Aug. 29-5-15. No 6712 Pte Kelly A returned off pass from England. No. 6332 Pte Wilde left for England on pass for U.K.9th. Despatched duplicate A.F. N1513 34 csc 65TAg Base these being for month of April.	

WAR DIARY
or
INTELLIGENCE SUMMARY.
(Erase heading not required.)

Army Form C. 2118.

Hour, Date, Place	Summary of Events and Information	Remarks and references to Appendices
Croix Du Bac. 4-7-15.	Met D.O.S. at Vieilleard at 11 am. by appointment. Reported to Corps in reply to yesterday's "that trials were being worked out, in view of being wanted" of a hyper-pression column when the possible trade of per batting." Reported new pattern pendulum sight and 2/Corps 2" trench improvement to beobachtes to and Army 1 rifle grenades. The above with a "in Army workshops. Application for 10 ball & hr. Sudden filler pick up for issue to 15 & 4 Batteries. Wired estimates for a 12 P.R. gun, wagon No 79 in charge of 133 Bde. was lost. Also to reserve for 4 F.A.R.	
5-7-15.	Attended demonstration on opening of smoke helmets afterwards arranged with A.D.M.S. Entry Army bearers up 3rd and 5th Army Plan O. bered to ventilation for damping. Received numerous drafts 1st. from 3" Corps for local issues same 15 Ambulance Col. also a L.P. Signalling Disc which was issued to C.R.A. for trial by a forward observing officer. Report to 3rd Corps on improved pendulum sight for rifle grenades not used in pursuance to original pattern. Brigades advise no L. officer watchmaker of second for of the grenades produced up to date. no Rifle grenade rest manufactured in the 2nd Army workshops.	

Army Form C. 2118.

WAR DIARY
or
INTELLIGENCE SUMMARY.
(Erase heading not required.)

Instructions regarding War Diaries and Intelligence Summaries are contained in F.S. Regs, Part II. and the Staff Manual respectively. Title pages will be prepared in manuscript.

Hour, Date, Place		Summary of Events and Information	Remarks and references to Appendices
CROIX DU BAC	6-7-15.	Received 1500 metres of canvas for Tactical screens from Ordnance 2nd Army and issued it to C.R.E. Three B.S.A. rifles fitted with Magnifying lens sights Nos 5455, 5718, 5628 were handed over by 80th Bde to 6 & 2nd to equalize the numbers in each Brigade on 4 limit.	
"	7-7-15	Allowed weekly expense of 2000 at 3rdCorps Report to 3rd Corps on proposed abolition of the cut off to facilitate production of rifles. Not recommended unless it will greatly facilitate output.	
"	8-7-15	Received 1800 smoke helmets on loan from GOC 12th Division Gravespeed under instructions received from DDOS 2nd Army. Report to 3rd Corps gun & half ammunition number of spare parts essential for efficient service of Vickers gun. Pointed out that if the parts are reduced it is essential MG should be ready for throwing from tree when required in stead of heavy travel of 4 to 6 weeks at present. Received 17 more portable waterlogs for Machine guns from 3rd Corps Issued remains 4 Catapults 3 to 8th Div 1 to 82nd Bde.	
"	9-7-15	Report on number of boots repaired by units from 1-1-15 to 30-6-15 sent to 88 OS. 2nd Army units did not consider the appointment of a boot inspector in the field would serve any useful purpose; quite agree. Report on shoe packs received for trial sent to 3rdCorps; impossible to test a boot satisfactorily in summer to see if it would suit all requirements for winter. Reports also on a latter, and fur lined waders. Wanted in such a hurry that often there is not time to test thoroughly by them.	

(73989) W4141—463. 400,000. 9/14. H.&J.Ltd. Forms/C. 2118/10.

WAR DIARY
or
INTELLIGENCE SUMMARY.
(Erase heading not required.)

Army Form C. 2118.

Instructions regarding War Diaries and Intelligence Summaries are contained in F.S. Regs., Part II and the Staff Manual respectively. Title pages will be prepared in manuscript.

Hour, Date, Place	Summary of Events and Information	Remarks and references to Appendices
CROIX DU BAC. 9-7-15	In this case recommended that troops of 1/5 should be issued to Battalion and 200 to Field Companies. If 1/5 arms issued to 1/5 have them in lieu of gun books. Reported on I.P. humane Lethan sent for trial by Corps H.Q. pistol: recommended were in replacement of Webleys. Total of 6 all revolvers which have no humane loops a 2 pr Bn promptly. Sent 2130 blades of Paris to be cleaned.	
10-7-15	Application for extra bolts, saddles for 2nd field Ambulance received. Took to 'Corps' not approved. 2nd Cambridgeshire Regt do not short Rifles and long bayonets to complete their establishment in exchange for long 203 bayonets & webbing effects Nos. Bis Armourers Shop. 50 Damaged short Rifles sent to 2nd Army Workshops for fitting to rests for firing. Hales rifle grenades. 4198 Sub Con & R. Rapple granted fur. to 11/7/15 to 17/7/15 to Ireland. Vacates abolition need an state for Bundle Helmets etc.	
11/7/15	Trucks withstores arriving irregularly. Prepared a list of bulk items issued to Battery funds and sent to C.R.A. called for explanation as to the numbers drawn by 9.5 1/3 Battery R.F.A. B285 2nd Army insist that 2000 rounds lebolaissance to be added one per 28 & gun as a temporary measure.	Per 0284-15 to 15-7-15 /6 weeks

WAR DIARY
or
INTELLIGENCE SUMMARY
(Erase heading not required.)

Army Form C. 2118.

Hour, Date, Place	Summary of Events and Information	Remarks and references to Appendices
CROIX DU BAC 12-7-15	Took 2 Sporting Rossi of motor B.S. on charge of "2nd Divisional" G.I.O.M. 2nd Corps for repair by 2nd Army F.P. Workshop Nos 47/15, 7491, 4796. Militarism Repairs of bags completed which were received from 2DTS. 2nd Army, for motor vehicles. Bill paid France 246-05 fr to 1027. 12 Battle sight for worm gears received from OC 3rd Corps.	
" 13-7-15	Received 39 Bicycles in bulk for Distribution to units. 1 withheld for A Battery 50th Bde Doubtown. Fetched 2000 Smoke Helmets from 5th DS. 2 " Bns or 2gs to be taken up & promptly by 2DS 11 Pont U. Issued 8 batteries Nos 6 for women, 4 each to 2nd & 10 Divisions & 1st Canadian and Received 3 Rifles with telescopic sights from OC 3rd Corps. 1st CAMBRIDGE regn DO instruct me now all equipped with these after being temporally loaned home to train all in details instructing men & June 1st	Nos of rifles P.3944 (not in town) P. 6362 P. 7337
" 14-7-15	Attended conference at 3rd Corps at Noon. 57 Bicycles ordered for trans only 25 turned up truck with remaining 26 was not up. Authorised for issue of Pistols illuminating 1/pistol with 10 per 3rd Inf Bde received lowe, 8 Bdes for indents. Also required for 4 pairs per Bn of Spectacles sniper for use in observing aeroplanes; and letter to each Brigade. Letter from corps calling for report as to sufficiency of musketry was in possession of units.	

WAR DIARY or INTELLIGENCE SUMMARY

Army Form C. 2118.

Hour, Date, Place	Summary of Events and Information	Remarks and references to Appendices
CROIX DU BAC 15-7-15	Reported Troops resufficiency of wire cutters received by increase 25.100 from Field Corps RE and 26 from Army Sig. Obtd. suits and greased a mounting system customary of Reg. Wag. Wire a tele. U. RE Park for issue when special operations take place. One Telescope rifle P.7976 received from OC 3"Corps. Despatched spring for time to 6/C Res. 3" Division. G.O.C. 4/6 Batteys command Sq. of 7" Corps. Tried wire cutters again and will arrive Balance of Acycles 26 arrived additional wire arrived.	
" 16-7-15	Wire received from 3"Corps Wor. No 2 Mountain Battery could leaflets for administration drawn from how mens issued. Helios Buzzers other not returned. 1 Bicycle sent up by base private to A.Botley 50"BDe (Balks accompanied (increase 61 up Scale.	
" 17-7-15	S/Cond. Royal reported off punt. from Fehin. D Returns 1" Army of trucks, Guns in presence of Units. One Maxim issued to 8" Div. Cuits in exchange for MKI Cavals etd. returns O.S.O Britain. Returns of Telephone o Cable return July to 3" Army. all telephones complete & Nota 91 & 62 & 79 3 Ch Bat. D in y transported HTD "17 AFD Note it. 1/d. Mo 91 15-ca flamers eng stops 15/6 of pair 130 Pat 2 of 80 Billioting officer. RMG 2376R received. of Railway Tunnel to transit of HTp which went disposed 78 Benett successful return of Trip to entrance allocated informed to hand on CALAIS	

WAR DIARY
or
INTELLIGENCE SUMMARY

(Erase heading not required.)

Army Form C. 2118.

Hour, Date, Place	Summary of Events and Information	Remarks and references to Appendices
Base O/00IX Du BAC 18-7-15	Raillard changed GIZAGORGUE would it to ascertain time of arrival and departure. Received orders to form 500 lb Garrison for No 2 Mountain Battery. Returned 32 saddles & Kadhus (reduced by 39 of Battery RFA being off saddles for Mhorses). No 5143 R/Corps Ptl C.D required Restoration auxiliary to service on return unused under present conditions.	
19-7-15	Proceeded to 2nd Army and deliver 9 th Accord for repair of smoke Helmets. Reply to 3rd Corps recommending issue of an extra Bags Tool Farriers filled to each company of the Train owing troops sections being off despatches. Report of 3rd Corps sent on treatment made GOC Signalling authorized. Great made by forward R.A. staking officer who reports opening to total inaccurate quick cutting suggested the same pattern close with a larger staff catching haste. Lower down to third could be used in a bad. We resumed form Indian as Communications that Captain ODD B O'y would relieve me. And that I was approved home as soon as possible after relief and reports to War office for duty. D.A.G. Base enquiring when and instructions. Notified by WK Base 1st Army towards Reynoldstonstin as a Garrison that the 19 H of Infantry Bde ceases to be attached to Garrison from tomorrow & will be attached to 8A Garrison.	OR/2950 dtd 19/7/15

(73989) W4141—463. 400,000. 9/14. H.&J.Ltd. Forms/C. 2118/10.

Army Form C. 2118.

WAR DIARY
or
INTELLIGENCE SUMMARY.
(Erase heading not required.)

Instructions regarding War Diaries and Intelligence Summaries are contained in F. S. Regs., Part II. and the Staff Manual respectively. Title pages will be prepared in manuscript.

Hour, Date, Place	Summary of Events and Information	Remarks and references to Appendices
CROIX DU BAC 20-7-15	Reply to 3rd Corps re drawers for Highland battalions from late issue. One battalion required none, other 2 recommended short-close fitting woollen drawers to come some 6 or 7 inches above the knee and provision of long hose tops to pull upon the knee. Instructions re issue about drawl of arms from return infty adv reserve after return NCO for MK VII action instructions issued with rifles after return NCO for MK VIII action instructions issued accordingly.	
" 21-7-15	Attended conference at 3rd Corps H.Q. hotspot supply refilling points would be changed tomorrow available for new dumps. Two returns arrived from Base for issue to "D" Co. Returns arrived to return two Vickers gun tripods Cambridge Regt undermounts to return two Vickers gun tripods to 7th Division.	
" 22-7-15	Visited the trenches at ENQUINING FEM and STEENWERCK to see if any government property had been deposited by battalions. Received one bandolier contg filled gun ammn Pure. Dropped three tongues for use of Chaplains of trg bns in garages to purchase some troops. Reprimanding Office 82nd Bde a/c for tram service. Reply to Corps re a report bag half waterproof cover and arm curtain for Balmoral. Boards are not covered ricean ay.	

WAR DIARY
or
INTELLIGENCE SUMMARY.
(Erase heading not required.)

Army Form C. 2118.

Instructions regarding War Diaries and Intelligence Summaries are contained in F.S. Regs., Part II and the Staff Manual respectively. Title pages will be prepared in manuscript.

Hour, Date, Place	Summary of Events and Information	Remarks and references to Appendices
Abbaye du BAC 22.7.15	Report as to sufficiency of the 2 scales for artillery with "and/or" 3rd Corps. Stating predecessor's sufficient for 18Pr Batteries. 9 Brigades but recommending an increase to 8 rounds for howitzer batteries. Received 5 Rifle Hyperscopes from OC 3rd Corps Troops (allotted to 82nd 3rd Bde)	
" 23.7.15	1° Consignment of rifles withdrawn from batteries was to-day 158 & sent to Base NQS. 0.5.13.16.13. 3 Telescopic Rifles retd V.5766 V.3427 V 3430. rec'd 1 Daylight signalling lamp, 1 case of Sulphuric acid (from R.A.) rec'd from OC 3rd Corps. Reported by 3 Corps on scarcity of relief tomb by Batteries of Infantry panniers not received — return of 3 a Doctor of B7 & Battalions 9 NCS 3 privates. Maxim Casualty gun NK released by issue of a Browning.	
" 24.7.15	Reply 6-0 3rd Corps regarding of empty ammunition cartridge cases in boxes for return. Base Damage challenge difficulty, and present cultivation and Gretnard culverts in use. No tried of bins from base. 2 Vickers guns handed in to Divn Armourer Shop. Relieved by issue of 2 Canadian Ross. A Clocking 7 in rapidity of strange 6-12 a Division.	

WAR DIARY
or
INTELLIGENCE SUMMARY.

(Erase heading not required.)

Army Form C. 2118.

Hour, Date, Place	Summary of Events and Information	Remarks and references to Appendices
CROIX DU BAC 25/7/15	Received Order to 3rd Corps re number of Dummy Grenades for training purposes which should be issued to Ifts. of each Battalion etc. also that 5 weekly reports of 50 hyposcopes to this and part two. 7 Telescopic rifles issued 6-150 number one last and part two. 3rd Corps wired that all Battalions are to be relieved at once.	80 H 81 H 82 nd 7976 3944 5766 3430 7537 3427 6562
" 26/7/15	Relief changed to FLEURBAIX. Orders it no strong enemy lookout (Kemmerbel pill) for PC col. Report sent to Corps on the 5 rifle hyposcopes recently received 82nd Bde reports unsuccessful experiments tried for trench warfare suggest slight alteration. Put up letter to Corps asking frantically for issue of 40 pairs of gumboots for use of guards in claying trenches. Shelters in area.	
" 27/7/15	46.25 Smoke Helmets received for troops towards receive of persian manipulate STIKI returned from 9th RScots on receipt of a paper relief to issue as about 36 rifles from Battalions on CBB 1613. Returned to Corps guing number for return indicating a portion after replacement under the authority.	

WAR DIARY
INTELLIGENCE SUMMARY
(Erase heading not required.)

Army Form C. 2118.

Hour, Date, Place	Summary of Events and Information	Remarks and references to Appendices
CROIX DU BAC 28-7-15	Delivered Sorden Make Trigger recd from 3rd Corps to 8 & 2nd Bde for trial against suspected French mortar 8 & 2nd Bde to found O.K. to be Hague pattern old pattern 3.7 inst 9/8 "vent". Recd back from 1st & 2nd Corps 2 Telescopes sighting and recg Sen 2 B.S.L Range finders belonging to 3rd Corps. Sense 6 is sent for repair. Attended conference 3rd Corps H.Q. Received 1 Tele: copic Rifle no U 5787 from 00 3rd Corps (allotted to 8 Bde) making 4 in possession of each Brigade. No 2 Mountain Battery H.Q. & Nº 10 Section all concerned informed.	no U 5787
29-7-15	Corps Commander visited dummies shops. Reported on necessity of stores for Trip ods and matters received from Brigades who all agreed in need & were not necessary. Report to Corps accordingly. Application put up to Corps asking for another 3 & P level meridians of possible to obtain. Capt ODDBOY McQuarry Bnd Sgt arrived from 2nd Army to take over in afternoon.	

Army Form C. 2118.

WAR DIARY
or
INTELLIGENCE SUMMARY.
(Erase heading not required.)

Instructions regarding War Diaries and Intelligence Summaries are contained in F.S. Regs., Part II and the Staff Manual respectively. Title pages will be prepared in manuscript.

Hour, Date, Place	Summary of Events and Information	Remarks and references to Appendices
CROIX DUBAC 30-7-15	Handing over order to Capt ODDBOY. Waterproof this Hangs Rubbed, 1 Jordan Cap and 4/- Rayfalon overcoat of 4/MR He Bode for repairs. Generated Batt. Armoured Ships	
"	Received Waterproofs for use in carrying injured in the Trenches. Total received £80 W/Sob for that purpose. Completes Handing over order to Capt C. ODDBOY.	

[signature]
Lieut Colonel
S.R.S.S.T
27th Div.

27th Division

Confidential

War Diary

of

D.A.D.O.S. 27th Division

From 1st August 1915 To 31st August 1915

(Volume III)

WAR DIARY or INTELLIGENCE SUMMARY

Hour, Date, Place	Summary of Events and Information	Remarks and references to Appendices
CROIX, du BAC. 1st August 1915	Lieut. Col. R.H. Hill left for England for duty at War Office. Report on trial of Borden Cable Trigger received from 5.25 Brigade forwarded to S. of Spr. The trigger is considered suitable for firing single shots from Rifle Battery. It could not be fitted to metal framed periscopes without modification.	
3rd August 1915	Phosphorescent sights aug.tt. be received and 32 issued to 80 and 82 Inf Brigades. Smoke helmets - notification received that no more repairs are to be undertaken locally. All defective helmets were to be sent to Base. Major W.H. Back A.D.Sgl. arrived from England to see working of sq division in the field.	

WAR DIARY
or
INTELLIGENCE SUMMARY.
(Erase heading not required.)

Army Form C. 2118.

Hour, Date, Place	Summary of Events and Information	Remarks and references to Appendices
CROIX DU BAC 3rd August 15	Accompanied by Major Buck master Rathens refilling point, Indian Corps workshops. Special sleeves received and handed over to RA for issue to the Brigade much in need of it. Issued to 36th Battery (6/6)	9/1
4th August 15	Started Rathens and Major Buck. Called at Ordnance Armourer's shop on return. Attended Conference at Head Quarters 3rd Corps. Nothing of importance from 1st London's - Portable machine Gun mounting. Heard from Bear's re Lawrence.	9/1
5th August 15	Major W Buck returned to England. Canvas Water Carrier - Report on trial sent to 3rd Corps. Carrier considered satisfactory and issue at the rate of 8 per Battery recommended -	9/1

Army Form C. 2118.

WAR DIARY
or
INTELLIGENCE SUMMARY.
(Erase heading not required.)

Hour, Date, Place	Summary of Events and Information	Remarks and references to Appendices
CROIX AU BAC 6th August 1915	Steel helmets for protection against shrapnel 40 were received from 3rd Corps and 2.0 were issued to the 80th and 82nd Brigades for trial and report.	
7th August 1915	Wrote 1st Army asking if Chayoux or Jardin syringes could be produced in Paris for the purpose of spraying manure heaps as a preventive against breeding of flies, also asking for information as to the Removal of Manure Contract.	
8th August 1915	Cent: water tank received from Base for 2nd Royal Irish Fusiliers. Eight pairs of binocular glasses received from Base, in lieu of Promoters for issue to 2nd D.C.L.I.	
9th August 1915	Eye fringes received from Base and issued to units. Lance Cpl Sadler proceed to England on 7 days leave.	

Army Form C. 2118.

WAR DIARY
or
INTELLIGENCE SUMMARY.
(Erase heading not required.)

Instructions regarding War Diaries and Intelligence Summaries are contained in F.S. Regs., Part II and the Staff Manual respectively. Title pages will be prepared in manuscript.

Hour, Date, Place	Summary of Events and Information	Remarks and references to Appendices
CROIX DU BAC 10th August 1915	The announcement of the Three Infantry Brigades brought in to Divisional Manoeuvre Staff — One Armr left with each Brigade for several armr.	
11th August 1915	Visited Conference of 3rd Corps: no point of importance brought forward.	46/
12th August 1915	Carriages, ambulance, stretchers received, wicket machine guns received from Base and seven 3rd Kings Royal Rifle Corps. Compressor Cavalry kymograph received in lieu of magneto and issues Units.	47/
13th August 1915	Further consignment of mark V binocular received from Base in lieu of Prismatic and issued to 2nd D.C.L.I.	48/

(73989) W4141—463. 400,000. 9/14. H.&J.Ltd. Forms/C. 2118/10.

WAR DIARY
or
INTELLIGENCE SUMMARY.
(Erase heading not required.)

Army Form C. 2118.

Instructions regarding War Diaries and Intelligence Summaries are contained in F.S. Regs., Part II. and the Staff Manual respectively. Title pages will be prepared in manuscript.

Hour, Date, Place	Summary of Events and Information	Remarks and references to Appendices
CROIX BAC 14th August 1915	Units sent to Armoury arranged for. Shells to be sent to Brigade HQ. Small arm ammunition to have doubts hope with about half hopes to be not more for orders to write for ditto. it is greener to prevent damage to removable objects.	
15th August 1915	Attended conference of staff 27 & envirom. Decided to continue old normal arrangements for present, no other point brought forward.	
16th August 1915	Private Walker relieved from Lewis machine gun allowance for 2nd R.I. brothers. Major N. Report on Steel helmet sent HQrs. 300 teams for small hopes, recommendation for as new slopes. O/C Brigade hetruck Authorities received from Brigade Issued 12 bond Battalion M.S. machine gun company. Private Dye placed 6 Brigades on 7 days leave.	

WAR DIARY
or
INTELLIGENCE SUMMARY.
(Erase heading not required.)

Army Form C. 2118.

Hour, Date, Place	Summary of Events and Information	Remarks and references to Appendices

CROIX DU BAC

17th August 1915 — Boon satchets for smoke helmets & new from Base no 37 smoke helmets to each [?]. Smoke helmet for moment — 1 ticker for from 2nd Shropshires reptd [?] returns [?]

18 August 1915 — Attended conference of CO's at Hqrs Rosta by G.O.C. In points that slightly hung up to [?] for gun-rifle grenades, and that some classes be arranged for officers, so as to explain various functions and uses. He is now for [?] trench [?].

19 August 1915 — Reports 6.30 G.S. that the name of our pregntations for each week were from Bailey was recommended. 2 wh light sent [?] from 3rd Batln and [?] [?] Strome to home 6.30 am Cpt Bn.Brn [?] have one report. 2 men slightly [?] mortar gunning from GH.S. on [?] [?]. 6.17 W.Batly enemy [?].

WAR DIARY or INTELLIGENCE SUMMARY

Army Form C. 2118.

Hour, Date, Place	Summary of Events and Information	Remarks and references to Appendices
CROIX DU BAC 20th August 1915	Three small storehouses taken over for the storage of smoke helmets and respirators. Application received from machine gun Battery 1st Defence Command, 6 Corps. Report sent that army different forwarded that there is only one Coy Gun due to wickness. 3rd Corps called for report of horse shoes etc can be made at locality. 375 smoke helmet tips station received. The counter is seven one waters for smoke helmets and 3,500 smoke helmets for smoke helmets. Report on lots Cart received from Base. Arrangement made with Iron receiver for rifle - @ 3rd Corps called relative 3rd Corps for report - @ 3rd Corps called relative to damaged rifles.	
21st August 1915	Metal belts for machine guns-report received from Lnf Brigades and draft prepared for 3rd Corps concerning of ammunition that these shoner not replace nell. Six Vickers guns '303" hyperaufes received from Base 1st Leinster Regt and R.97.	

WAR DIARY
INTELLIGENCE SUMMARY
(Erase heading not required.)

Army Form C. 2118.

Hour, Date, Place	Summary of Events and Information	Remarks and references to Appendices
CROIX DU BAC 22nd August 1915	Maximum fire received and sent to good R.F.'s etc. Originals of R.S.M 1513 forwarded to Command Paymaster.	
23rd August 1915	Base — Instructions received to withdraw protabs and equipment from Surplus Rangetaker, return same to the Base and issue rifles and equipment in lieu. This is consequent on 1 man Rangefinder not being available for issue in full.	
24th August 1915	Approval Received for the issue of Periscope Hyposcope to Head Quarters of artillery Brigade in the proportion of one per Brigade. Owing to scarcity of Service pattern bicycles it was intimated that had fallen wires to supplier in lieu — Instructions issued that empty tins would with grenades were to be collected and handed over to R.E. Attended Conference at 3rd Inf. Head Quarters. Nothing Special to record.	

WAR DIARY or INTELLIGENCE SUMMARY.

(Erase heading not required.)

Army Form C. 2118.

Hour, Date, Place	Summary of Events and Information	Remarks and references to Appendices
6.20.14 am Btc 25th August 1915	Smoke helmet tube pattern priority of issue 6 be as under- Machine Gunners, Officers, NCOs and men - Satchels for smoke helmets slings to be modified by making extra button holes.	
26th August 1915	Report on Note Division optical sight received from 5th and 51st Infantry Brigades and transmitted to 3rd Corps. The sights are considered [satisfactory and] recommendation at the rate of 16 for each Battalion.	
27th August 1915	Regimental Paymaster Woolwich confirms that the allotment of pay made by Private Wilne 1st Regiment No 6337 to ten pence and not one [penny] as shown in pay book.	
28th August 15	Issue of blankets on the scale of one per man approved - 31,000 demanded from base accordingly. Shelling.	

Army Form C. 2118.

WAR DIARY
or
INTELLIGENCE SUMMARY.
(Erase heading not required.)

Instructions regarding War Diaries and Intelligence Summaries are contained in F.S. Regs., Part II. and the Staff Manual respectively. Title pages will be prepared in manuscript.

Hour, Date, Place	Summary of Events and Information	Remarks and references to Appendices
CROIX DU BAC 29th August 1915	Instructions received from 1st Army that badges and letters for Territorials are to be the same as those supplied to Regular units of the same arm.	
30th August 1915	To prevent slavery to rifle by firing, grenade approval was given for 16 rifles to be set aside for each Battalion for this purpose. Slightly bulged bulged barrels of rifles.	
31st August 1915	The question of the renunciation of stores for machine guns having been completely cognisant of the concerns of opinion is that no regulation can be made. Report to 3rd Corps accordingly. No A of bySS. Lt Capt Juding answers to information given only now. Ecauther Captain	

27th Division

Confidential

War Diary
of
D.A.D.O.S 27th Division
From 1st September 15 To 30 September 1915

Volume IV

M

WAR DIARY
or
INTELLIGENCE = SUMMARY.
(Erase heading not required.)

Army Form C. 2118.

Hour, Date, Place	Summary of Events and Information	Remarks and references to Appendices
CROIX DU BAC 1st September 1915	Intimation received that it was hoped to issue tents and to unwaterproof ground- sheets equipment on the following scale. Strength 25,20 tents hospital, marquees 35/20=— Latrine buckets 840 Keep nets one portable for lighting 200 Resistor Rowmore – Intended Infantry Shops.	
2nd September 1915	Cats for Light Hydraulic & New Brands Provides of ropes for some encountered as to how tents be tent—	
3rd September 1915	Confidential reference from 27 Divisional Ammunition (Column) that 20 H.E. Shrapnel received with Regiment was filled that those which were dangerous. Arranged for such tops to be filled locally.	49

Army Form C. 2118.

WAR DIARY
or
INTELLIGENCE SUMMARY.
(Erase heading not required.)

Instructions regarding War Diaries and Intelligence Summaries are contained in F. S. Regs., Part II. and the Staff Manual respectively. Title pages will be prepared in manuscript.

Hour, Date, Place	Summary of Events and Information	Remarks and references to Appendices
CROIX-DU-BAC 4th September 1915	Information received that the purchase of potatoes in England was strongly forbidden and that applications for refunds of the value of stores so purchased could not be considered.	92
5th September 1915	The provision of officers acting as Town Mayors, R.O.O. sanctioned and extra duty pay at 7/- per day approved under the terms of the R.W. while performing the duties of A.A. and Q.M.G.	93
6th September 1915	Battery one night. In response to a report called for by the A.A. it was recommended that eight officers and eight B.n.s ought to be issued to each Battalion of Infantry.	94

WAR DIARY or INTELLIGENCE SUMMARY

Army Form C. 2118.

Hour, Date, Place	Summary of Events and Information	Remarks and references to Appendices
CRDIX DHQ BAC 7th September 1915	No. 6755 Pte Furlong returned from leave. No. 7659 Pte Kirkham granted leave.	
8 September 1915	Decision received from 3rd Corps in reply to question raised by R.A. that Army Form B.109 8/10 was applicable to units of the New Army only owing to sufficiently informing on the letter it has been decided to affix titles of the employer etc. Conference at Headquarters 3rd Corps nothing of note occurred.	
9 September 1915	Conagin tenders approved for issue to troops. R.F.A. Bomb Throwers up to 25 rounds of 5" trench mortar.	
10 September 1915	Instructions received that it has been decided to abolish the uncertain designation of the 27th Ind Division Ammunition Columns.	

WAR DIARY
INTELLIGENCE SUMMARY
(Erase heading not required.)

Army Form C. 2118.

Hour, Date, Place	Summary of Events and Information	Remarks and references to Appendices
CROIX DU BAC 11th September 1915	Notified that a N.C.O. rendered unfit to be sent from England to join the Squadron for employment in the duties of Brigade Scoffeer. Submitted application to Divisional staff for authority to write off certain stores sent upon Squadron but necessarily abandoned in Ypres before issue could be made.	
12th September 1915	Intimation received that damaged harness were available at the Base for the purpose of obtaining back or recovery to horses received.	
13th September 1915	Instructed the exchange of wagons & to be charge of the S.S.M. hat a working party of 2 wagons, 1 Commander, 1 S. N.C.O. & 8 men Shoulder proceed and worked to the Base accordingly.	

WAR DIARY
or
INTELLIGENCE SUMMARY.

(Erase heading not required.)

Army Form C. 2118.

Hour, Date, Place	Summary of Events and Information	Remarks and references to Appendices
CROIX DU BAC 1st September 1915	Left Bayenghem for the purpose of finding water for hints during the next two months. No 5145 L/Cpl Peck and No 7659 Pte Gilkes reported from to-day. Instructions received that all full blankets of Each Brigade withdrawn and stored at Steenwerck prior to transfer to new area.	
MERRIS. 16th September 1915	Office closed at CROIX DU BAC and opened at MERRIS. Smoke Helmets taken to Steenbecque Railway Station in readiness for entrainment to new area. (Blankets of 83rd Inf Brigade still stored at Steenwerck)	

WAR DIARY
or
INTELLIGENCE SUMMARY.
(Erase heading not required.)

Army Form C. 2118.

Hour, Date, Place	Summary of Events and Information	Remarks and references to Appendices
MERRIS. 17th September 1915	Blankets of 91st Brigade withdrawn and after a return to Steenwerck. The blankets of the 80th Brigade were conveyed from Steenwerck by lorries. Supplies of Gas. to HAZEBROUCK for entrainment for transfer to new armies.	
MERRIS. 18th September 1915	1st & 10th stores left and travelled down with advanced section of Supply Column. Arrived at 5.30 p.m.	
MARFUSEE 19th September 1915	Lorries arrived with stores from all areas. An Army call for return showing employment, park of lorries and carriages required to complete spare to approved scale. D.D.O.S. 3rd Army called to ascertain if we were satisfactory on arriving in area & to	

WAR DIARY
or
INTELLIGENCE SUMMARY.
(Erase heading not required.)

Army Form C. 2118.

Instructions regarding War Diaries and Intelligence Summaries are contained in F.S. Regs., Part II. and the Staff Manual respectively. Title pages will be prepared in manuscript.

Hour, Date, Place	Summary of Events and Information	Remarks and references to Appendices
WARFUSÉE 20th September	The cart for No 2 on O.S. 18 pdr carriages to be modified only as may be necessary and units informed accordingly	
MERICOURT 20th September 15 – 22nd September 15	20 magazines per division sanctioned for use in advance bn tercing pots – Indent for gun parts to be renewed to prevent duplicate issues. Defectopants to be collected and sent to workshops. 4 Oserinnal spanges received and comes as bench stores	
23rd September 1915	Decided that the pocket anzyferdor was not sufficiently accurate to prevent accidents from sight spring bunds thrown out. Eight balance catchpests authorized for each division theirg on Am Invertedly	

(73959) W41411—463. 400,000. 9/14. H.&J.Ltd. Forms/C. 2118/10.

WAR DIARY
or
INTELLIGENCE SUMMARY.

(Erase heading not required.)

Army Form C. 2118.

Hour, Date, Place	Summary of Events and Information	Remarks and references to Appendices
HERICOURT 24th September 1915	Establuc Emitelescope on the scale of 8 per Battalion sanctioned. Firing machines at the rate of 4 per Infantry Battalion on changes.	
25th September 1915	Officers received for the issue of additional Chronometers to complete to 4 per Battalion so as to allow of one here of issue to 6 each machine gun. Visited Amiens relative to the purchase of tools for baths and hand carts for French Batteries. Collected 20 megaphones from Beauval, 2 Army heavy workshops and 1000 yards of canvas from 1st Army for hospitals for use as screens. Range for Revolver to be worn by all attached to Brigade HQ Officers. Communicate to decide standard of efficiency. Battery of ant Machine Guns to be drawn from 5th Division Arty.	
26th September 1915		

Army Form C. 2118.

WAR DIARY
or
INTELLIGENCE SUMMARY.
(Erase heading not required.)

Instructions regarding War Diaries and Intelligence Summaries are contained in F. S. Regs., Part II. and the Staff Manual respectively. Title pages will be prepared in manuscript.

Hour, Date, Place	Summary of Events and Information	Remarks and references to Appendices
MERICOURT 27th September 1915	20 Rings/Packing - Disks patent - 073/15/2. with packing washer received for same. Visited Divns and purchased essential boilers for baths to Establishment. Report received that No 03755 Sergt Macfarlane had been evacuated to the Base suffering from acute Rheumatism	
28th September 1915	Visited 8th Army workshop and collected neophosms to Divns, calling at Divns to collect lids for bath and boiler for the same, these being too awkward of heating apparatus essential for providing hot water.	
29th September 1915	600 Knob screws no 2 co used k sent Infantry Bde.	

Army Form C. 2118.

WAR DIARY
or
INTELLIGENCE SUMMARY.
(Erase heading not required.)

Hour, Date, Place	Summary of Events and Information	Remarks and references to Appendices
MERICOURT 30th September 1915	Eighth Reinforcement from Thomas Reserves and two men to Bomb School. 276 Sent 6th received for Division, with a supply of tools. Butter for Cooking, 1lb. of cheese per and half lb. of bread for each tent etc. Browns Box inspected. Scarab Major LT DCJ 27/9/15	

Instructions regarding War Diaries and Intelligence Summaries are contained in F.S. Regs., Part II. and the Staff Manual respectively. Title pages will be prepared in manuscript.

12/7599

D.A.D.O.S. 27th Div.

Dec 1915

Vol I

Army Form C. 2118.

WAR DIARY
or
INTELLIGENCE SUMMARY.
(Erase heading not required.)

Instructions regarding War Diaries and Intelligence Summaries are contained in F.S. Regs., Part II. and the Staff Manual respectively. Title pages will be prepared in manuscript.

Hour, Date, Place	Summary of Events and Information	Remarks and references to Appendices
MERICOURT 1st October 1915	Further supply of GS shed prevent night eights received for distribution. 50 tons stores received from Base for distribution to post for the Divisions occupying trenches. There are no other available troops attached to the Division.	
2nd October 1915	250 young soldiers received and posted to Battalions.	
3rd October 1915	Attention of commanding officers invited to the necessity of getting clothing looking to enable each man underclothing to be worn. Attention called to the necessity of paying attention to fitting and to condition of socks, as a preventive against trench feet. Issue on arrival likely to be taken by more than will the Division.	
4th October 1915	Information received from the Base that the First of the Drafts for a numbers Hostile Division are to ...	

Army Form C. 2118.

WAR DIARY
or
INTELLIGENCE SUMMARY.
(Erase heading not required.)

Instructions regarding War Diaries and Intelligence Summaries are contained in F. S. Regs., Part II and the Staff Manual respectively. Title pages will be prepared in manuscript.

Hour, Date, Place	Summary of Events and Information	Remarks and references to Appendices
MERICOURT 5th October 1915	Visited Amiens to procure costumes for observers and procured some from Zenghers & Co. Visited Section de Camouflage, Equipe G.N. attended conference at Head Quarters. Telegt of M/S that W Duncan workshops cleaned and is shop to be started again as soon as possible. Went to Ham Head Quarters relative to the provision of special clothing for men employed in my unit. Came here to their process for somewhat an to R.M.M. personnel trained & now. F.G.H.Q.	See [sig]
6th October 1915	[illegible handwritten text]	[sig]
7th October 1915	[illegible handwritten text]	[sig]

WAR DIARY
or
INTELLIGENCE SUMMARY.
(Erase heading not required.)

Army Form C. 2118.

Hour, Date, Place	Summary of Events and Information	Remarks and references to Appendices
MERICOURT 10 October 1915	Acting B.M. Sgt Marsh appointed acting B.M. conductor from 1/9/15, and wine a Report sent to 13 Corps showing think - was not long of ye	
16 October 1915	Divisional Artillery Report that usual supply to Divisions was setting some of to Yssapt(?) up [illegible] but four of short term out to be issued for the [illegible] out [illegible]	
11 October 1915	Plenty of supply of water issued 82nd Bgde temporarily attached also 6.0.2.0. from in charging places with 67th Dyy Bde for telescopes sighted after (learned) from 13 Corps. 100 Rounds ammunition from 13 Divisions	

Army Form C. 2118.

WAR DIARY
or
INTELLIGENCE SUMMARY.
(Erase heading not required.)

Instructions regarding War Diaries and Intelligence Summaries are contained in F. S. Regs., Part II. and the Staff Manual respectively. Title pages will be prepared in manuscript.

Hour, Date, Place	Summary of Events and Information	Remarks and references to Appendices
MERICOURT 12th October 1915	Scale of winter clothing published. Instructions relative to antigas appliances received from R.O. Notification received from Base that run book were not available for issue to officers. Ten Russian wire Cutters received from D.O.	GRO 1201 ARO.
13th October 1915	12 Cape Snoots for trial. Care of Arms. Attention called to the fact that subjecting bayonets to tent is unsuitable to render them useless as a fighting weapon.	
14th October 1915	Scale of Special winter clothing (faces) Scale of Bougres Secs at 400 p. Division. Notification received from Base that frost Caps would not be available before the 1st November - Frost hoods were available if wanted.	GRO 1204 " 1209

Army Form C. 2118.

WAR DIARY
or
INTELLIGENCE SUMMARY.
(Erase heading not required.)

Instructions regarding War Diaries and Intelligence Summaries are contained in F.S. Regs., Part II. and the Staff Manual respectively. Title pages will be prepared in manuscript.

Hour, Date, Place	Summary of Events and Information	Remarks and references to Appendices
M: BICOURT 15th October 1915	Scale of heel ropes to be increased to 50%. Stockholm approves for issue at the rate of 50 for each Battalion of Infantry for trial and report.	2y
16th October 1915	Nothing to record.	2y
17th October 1915	Amended scale of signalling panniers issued. Scale of rugs for Motor Cars approved. Scale of rifles fitted with telescopic sights and special sights for rifle grenades for each Battalion of Infantry.	GR.O.1219 GR.O.1220
18th October 1915.	Intimation received that it was proposed to issue from the Base lubricating oil in gallon drums. The rigid of issue was not commented as such issues were liable to lead to waste especially with small units. The following men not lower drawer on 17th inst. 039/17 Pte Taylor W; 0580/9 Rifleman C, mm 09236, Pte	2y

(73989) W.4141—463. 400,000. 9/14. H.&J.Ltd. (Forms/C. 2118/10.—7

WAR DIARY
INTELLIGENCE SUMMARY

(Erase heading not required.)

Army Form C. 2118.

Hour, Date, Place	Summary of Events and Information	Remarks and references to Appendices
MERICOURT 19th October 1915	Report received that water was being contaminated by the troops using miscellaneous pails &c for drawing water. Wooden buckets ordered for use on large wells in area.	
26th October 1915.	Smoke helmets tube pattern scale fixed at 3 per man, 2 to be carried on the man and one in Divisional Reserve. Smoke helmets made of any other material to be withdrawn from the men and replaced by others from the reserve. War diaries to be sent to the Officer i/c Adjutant General's office at the Base and not by O.C. A.G. Records. French mortar batteries. Issue of 1 2 ngs Roy No 17 approved.	
31st October	New form and Jumbar report to be rendered after one months trial and subsequently after 3 months one. W7SSR/6 Finding. 6332. Possible the after 3 months for boxes in England	

WAR DIARY
INTELLIGENCE SUMMARY
(Erase heading not required.)

Army Form C. 2118.

Instructions regarding War Diaries and Intelligence Summaries are contained in F. S. Regs., Part II. and the Staff Manual respectively. Title pages will be prepared in manuscript.

Hour, Date, Place	Summary of Events and Information	Remarks and references to Appendices
MERICOURT 22nd October 1915	Russian wire cutters sent to 96th Infy Brigade for trial for experimental report on. The pattern cannot be used with bayonet fixed unless the bayonet is in new cut or modified slightly by putting a notch in the bayonet or new cut of the rifle. Some recommended at the rate of 6 per cent of rifles with Battalion. Scanners aspiralling. Report sent 6 copies. That those were more complete report expected. Number of NCOs, Buglers, pioneers in training to complete artillery in training. Report sent to 3rd Army that the storehouses are not in 27th Division in 29th Division. Four wagons carry rifles in 27th Division. Ammunition received from 129th Brigade Amm. Column to replace shell. Gs sent to train. G.	
23rd October 1915	No stores from Base. Tents and sheets etc sent to Base to form Rest camp. Instructions received that the tents issued from 13 Corps were to be collected and returned to 3rd Army. Brigade Supply officer of Suffolks Stafford with Royal Welch Fusiliers.	

(73989) W4141—463. 400,000. 9/14. H.&J.L.Ld. Forms/C. 2118/10.

Army Form C. 2118.

WAR DIARY
INTELLIGENCE SUMMARY.
(Erase heading not required.)

Instructions regarding War Diaries and Intelligence Summaries are contained in F.S. Regs, Part II. and the Staff Manual respectively. Title pages will be prepared in manuscript.

Hour, Date, Place	Summary of Events and Information	Remarks and references to Appendices
MERICOURT 21st Oct 1915	No stores from Base. Division on the move. Instructions received to close at MERICOURT at 9am on 25/10/15 and open in new area. Same. No 052249 Cpl Perry No 81 Coy on Divisional duty.	
9am 25th October 15 MERICOURT	Left for new area.	
23am 25th Octr 15 BOVELLES.	Arrived from old area. No stores from Base and nothing to report.	
26th Octr 1915	Started Bovet relative to clothing and at Rest camp - Villers Bretonneux relative to storage of trench and river stores. 12 Offs relative to tent issue to Bovet Railway and Army relative to storage and disposal of the above. Cases of heavy breakage relative to adaptors for Tube and collected 6 for same to Genl HQ Havres.	

Army Form C. 2118.

WAR DIARY
INTELLIGENCE SUMMARY.
(Erase heading not required.)

Instructions regarding War Diaries and Intelligence Summaries are contained in F.S. Regs., Part II. and the Staff Manual respectively. Title pages will be prepared in manuscript.

Hour, Date, Place	Summary of Events and Information	Remarks and references to Appendices
BOUELLES, 27th October 15	Nothing to report. Division in rest area.	
28th Octr '15	Visited BOVES relative to striking camp equipment. Tents to conveyed to and placed in store as a temporary measure.	
29th Oct '15	Nothing to report.	
30th Oct '15	Nothing to report.	
31st Oct '15	Nothing to report.	

Scanbury Major
St AHQ 27 KR

D.A.D.O.S. 27th Div.

Nov.

Vol VI

121
7721

CONFIDENTIAL

War Diary
of
D.A.D.O.S. 27th Division

From 1st to 30th November 1915

Vol. 2

Army Form C. 2118.

WAR DIARY
or
INTELLIGENCE SUMMARY.
(Erase heading not required.)

Instructions regarding War Diaries and Intelligence Summaries are contained in F.S. Regs., Part II and the Staff Manual respectively. Title pages will be prepared in manuscript.

Hour, Date, Place	Summary of Events and Information	Remarks and references to Appendices
BOVELLES: 1st November 15	Great coats to be withdrawn when coats sheepskin lined are issued to M.T. Drivers. Artillery to be issued with rifles to complete to E. & E. 1098. Gas tube helmet to be taken by Division packed in bulk. Supply of Gloves - voided and lobe ones received see from Bases. Caps and trenches for frost caps - lydeaus called for and issued. Trousers & Braces Suppliers in bulk.	
2nd Nov. 1915.		
3rd Nov. 1915	Information received that the output of Glycerine is restricted and that the moment stock must be not used for refrigeration Gas apparatus. 960 great coats Cardigan required from troops. 1500 watched for Troops Telegs to Army Hg. Now. Reinforcement those for under clothing - how. 6 to College from several Battns. RFA. 6 to College from several obtaining collected and sent by ??? Smyth. Supply of Solatio by Smyth Received in ?? 3rd College ?? ?????? ????? from	
4th Nov 1915		

WAR DIARY
INTELLIGENCE SUMMARY

Army Form C. 2118.

Hour, Date, Place	Summary of Events and Information	Remarks and references to Appendices
BOUELLES 5th Nov 1915	Cable Service Dress due from Base Cancelled Consequent on the issue of winter Service Dress	
6th Nov 1915	Further supply of winter clothing received. New Boots Special pattern right deficiency of supply. 13 Specimens received from the new Equipment Ordnance Establishment Hope Romsey to be adjusted by Army. Another and other not available not to be taken - otherwise must all the equipment etc. A.F.B.198 renders. One instance has been to be packed in bulk. Shaw and marks of the Unit except Boots is to be taken. Also into the Camp Kettles & barrow to receive Cook arrangement on Cookers being withdrawn from Battalions.	
7th Nov 1915	Further supply of winter clothing received from Base. 450 Camp Kettles received to complete French Pattern transport 650 Lgts. By now decided that all water to are to are to be carried by	
8th Nov 1915	Supply of cap water Service Dress Serenes from Base. Inm intimate that the above additional smoke helmet Orders be remedied Base indent outstanding	

WAR DIARY
or
INTELLIGENCE SUMMARY.
(Erase heading not required.)

Army Form C. 2118.

Hour, Date, Place	Summary of Events and Information	Remarks and references to Appendices
Somilles 9th Nov 1915	Instructions received from 3rd Army to transfer 6 Cunards Ambulance Stretcher Mules. James Ballon age 40 Batteries tent pitching to 5th and 6th Divisions respectively. Instructions that noted for 16 wagons limbers to RE Regiment for RE unit to Doullens from Base. Night supply of Cape brute received from Base.	
10th Nov 15	Nothing to record	
11th Nov 15	Another supply of Cape mules received from Base 200 Shropshire Mules sent received from Havre.	
12th Nov 15	Another supply of Cape mules received from Calais.	

WAR DIARY or INTELLIGENCE SUMMARY

Army Form C. 2118.

Hour, Date, Place	Summary of Events and Information	Remarks and references to Appendices
BOVELLES 13th November/15	Decoration received from the 3rd Army that my photos should be sent for purposes of murder, and that copies should be furnished as shewn. Instructions from the Shops and sent to Paris for cleaning prior to repair. Nothing received from Sous Colonel McDonnell. Visited Divison.	
14th November/15	Truck supply of codes etc. ammunition and tel body recover from base. Four lorries began to recover from base and were sent to and from Divisions Signal Company.	
15th November/15	Left BOVELLES for MARSEILLES at 5.15pm. Sub Constn Coy marched and two Clark 6 follow. Prior to leaving asked S.D.W. if signal remain with Division for two days to complete issues prior to leaving to proceed on 15th November.	

(73989) W4141—463. 400,000. 9/14. H.&J.Ltd. Forms/C. 2118/10.

WAR DIARY
or
INTELLIGENCE SUMMARY.
(Erase heading not required.)

Army Form C. 2118.

Hour, Date, Place	Summary of Events and Information	Remarks and references to Appendices
MARSEILLES 16th November 15	Arrived at 9 am Reported to Base Comdt. to Cop. Base. interviewed at D.S.S. Lof. C. Nothing at depot for Division except a small quantity of Ammunition Shed has now set aside.=	
17th Nov 15"	No news of anything for Division – 4th Bde. arrived and Embarked – Interviewed OC relative to Equipment – Capes nocked hat hated and contains other items of Winter Clothing not yet received from Base, otherwise all Satisfactory.	
18th Nov 15	Notification received that catapulse had left Havre for Marseilles. Horses arrived. 3rd K.R.R. & 4th K.R.R. 2nd D.C.L.I. arrived and Embarked. Informed C.O. and M.L. Agent that no Winter clothing to complete issue was Required otherwise Equipment was Complete	

Army Form C. 2118.

WAR DIARY
or
INTELLIGENCE SUMMARY.
(Erase heading not required.)

Instructions regarding War Diaries and Intelligence Summaries are contained in F.S. Regs., Part II and the Staff Manual respectively. Title pages will be prepared in manuscript.

Hour, Date, Place	Summary of Events and Information	Remarks and references to Appendices
MARSEILLES – 19th Novr 1915	Notification received that stores had left Havre, also that coinage was to be purchased by C.O. MARSEILLES for issue to Batteries – No stores have yet arrived for Anyox in 80th Brigade two wires	
20th Novr 1915	Nothing to report –	
21st Novr 1915	Nothing to report	
22nd Novr 1915	Nothing to report	
23rd Novr 1915	Nothing to report	
24th Novr 1915	Nothing to report	Base quote No 6>8>2 6
25th Novr 1915	Stores received from Havre. Nothing to report.	
26th Novr 1915	Stores received from Havre in trucks No 49854, 56736, 140844. Nothing special to report.	
27th Novr 1915	Stores received from Base truck No 83/87 and 6952 – Telegraphed to Suzanne sent O.C. requesting that L. Rappel might be sent on and to forward so St Augure. To Boule and Duve waters from 81st & 82nd Supply Divisions (?Mea)........ 81st Bn have arrived.	

(73989) W4141—463. 400,000. 9/14. H.&J.Ltd. Forms/C. 2118/10.

Army Form C. 2118.

WAR DIARY
or
INTELLIGENCE SUMMARY.
(Erase heading not required.)

Instructions regarding War Diaries and Intelligence Summaries are contained in F. S. Regs., Part II. and the Staff Manual respectively. Title pages will be prepared in manuscript.

Hour, Date, Place	Summary of Events and Information	Remarks and references to Appendices
MARSEILLES. 28th November 1915	Divisional Head Quarters intimate that Etaps. Repple cannot be sent on as issues are to traced for troops not coming forward. Intimation received from Ordnance 3rd Army that under the terms of war office letter No 121/Stores/3905 (Q.M.G) dated 18th November 1915 that certain items of winter clothing required to complete that necessary to scale would be issued on arrival at destination.	
29th Nov/ 915	Stores received from Base. Truck No 40385	
36th Nov 15	Divisional Head Quarters as to total formations. Stores sent here for Divisional Train should be consigned.	

Scarsbury Major
Staff/R.A.S.C.
L.C.C.R.

www.ingramcontent.com/pod-product-compliance
Lightning Source LLC
Chambersburg PA
CBHW081241170426
43191CB00034B/2004